COUNTRY GENTLEMEN

Cherry Lane Music Company
Director of Publications/Project Editor: Mark Phillips

ISBN 1-57560-751-4

Copyright © 2004 Cherry Lane Music Company
International Copyright Secured   All Rights Reserved

The music, text, design and graphics in this publication are protected by copyright law. Any duplication or transmission, by any means, electronic, mechanical, photocopying, recording or otherwise, is an infringement of copyright.

Visit our website at www.cherrylane.com

CONTENTS

4	**Amazed**	*Lonestar*
9	**Bigger Than the Beatles**	*Joe Diffie*
14	**Down on the Farm**	*Tim McGraw*
17	**I Just Want to Dance with You**	*George Strait*
22	**I Like It, I Love It**	*Tim McGraw*
27	**I Love You This Much**	*Jimmy Wayne*
32	**I'm from the Country**	*Tracy Byrd*
38	**Let's Make Love**	*Tim McGraw*
45	**Maybe We Should Just Sleep on It**	*Tim McGraw*
50	**Meat & Potato Man**	*Alan Jackson*
54	**My Maria**	*Brooks & Dunn*
59	**Not a Day Goes By**	*Lonestar*
64	**Not That Different**	*Collin Raye*
69	**She's Taken a Shine**	*John Berry*
74	**Paint Me a Birmingham**	*Tracy Lawrence*
78	**She's Got It All**	*Kenny Chesney*
84	**She's My Kind of Rain**	*Tim McGraw*
88	**Smile**	*Lonestar*
92	**Stay Gone**	*Jimmy Wayne*
97	**This Used to Be Our Town**	*Jason McCoy*
102	**You Are**	*Jimmy Wayne*
108	**Your Everything**	*Keith Urban*

Amazed

Words and Music by
Chris Lindsey, Marv Green
and Aimee Mayo

*Recorded a half step lower.

Copyright © 1998 Songs Of Nashville DreamWorks (BMI), Careers-BMG Music Publishing, Inc. (BMI),
Silverkiss Music Publishing (BMI), Warner-Tamerlane Publishing Corp. (BMI) and Golden Wheat Music (BMI)
Worldwide Rights for Songs Of Nashville DreamWorks Administered by Cherry River Music Co.
Worldwide Rights for Silverkiss Music Publishing Administered by Careers-BMG Music Publishing, Inc.
Worldwide Rights for Golden Wheat Music Administered by Warner-Tamerlane Publishing Corp.
International Copyright Secured   All Rights Reserved

Bigger Than the Beatles

Words and Music by
Steve Dukes and Jeb Anderson

Copyright © 1995 DreamWorks Songs (ASCAP), Timbuk One Music (ASCAP),
Chickasaw Roan Music (ASCAP) and EMI Full Keel Music Co. (ASCAP)
Worldwide Rights for DreamWorks Songs Administered by Cherry Lane Music Publishing Company, Inc.
International Copyright Secured   All Rights Reserved

Down on the Farm

Verse 2:
Ed's been on a tractor, ain't seen Becky all week;
Somebody said they'd seen 'em headed down to the creek.
Farmer Johnson's daughter just pulled up in a Jeep,
Man, he knows how to grow 'em if you know what I mean.
Ol' Dave's gettin' loud but he don't mean no harm,
We're just country boys and girls gettin' down on the farm.
(To Chorus:)

Verse 3:
Well you can come as you are, there ain't no dress code,
Just some rural route rules that you need to know.
Don't mess with the bull, he can get real mean,
Don't forget to shut the gate, stay out of the beans.
If it starts to rainin' we'll just head to the barn,
We're country boys and girls gettin' down on the farm.
(To Chorus:)

I Just Want to Dance with You

Words and Music by
Roger Cook and John Prine

I Like It, I Love It

Words and Music by
Steve Dukes, Markus Anthony Hall
and Jeb Anderson

Copyright © 1995 DreamWorks Songs (ASCAP), EMI Full Keel Music (ASCAP), Lehsem Music, LLC (ASCAP) and Publishing Two's Music (ASCAP)
Worldwide Rights for DreamWorks Songs Administered by Cherry Lane Music Publishing Company, Inc.
Rights for Lehsem Music, LLC and Publishing Two's Music Administered by Music & Media International, Inc.
International Copyright Secured   All Rights Reserved

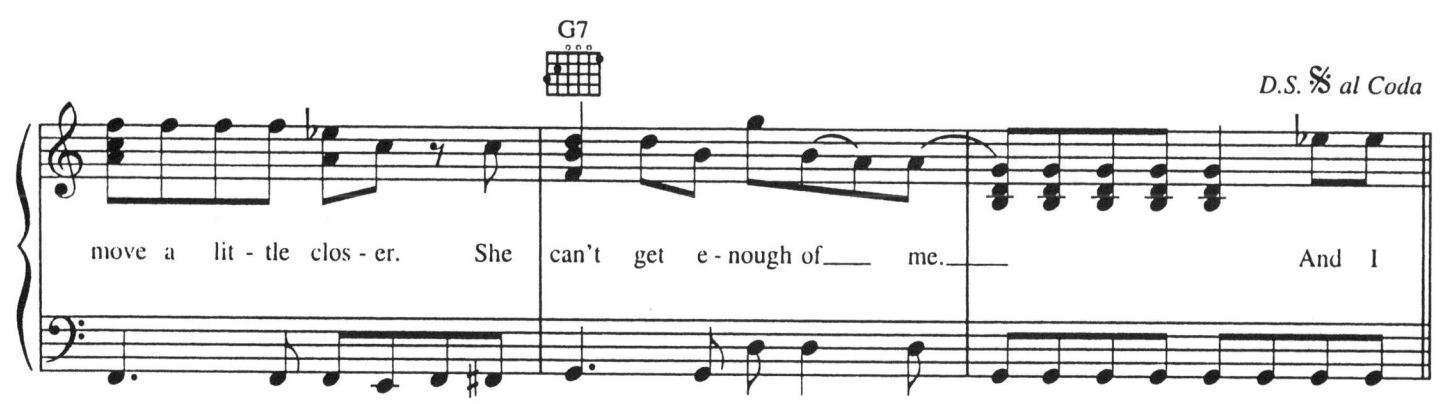

25

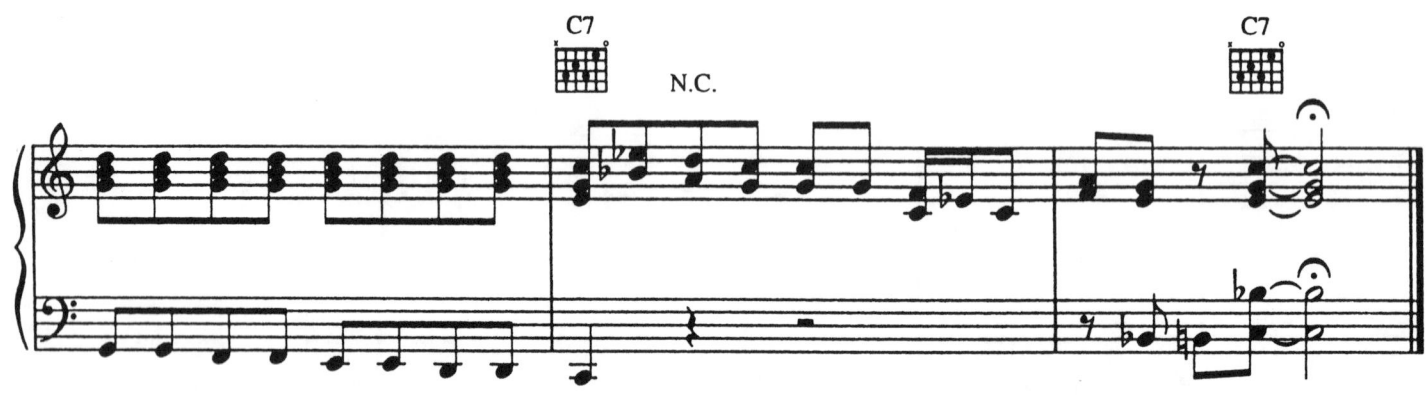

Verse 2:
My mama and daddy tried to teach me courtesy,
But it never sank in till that girl got a hold of me.
Now I'm holdin' up umbrellas and I'm openin' up doors,
I'm takin' out trash and I'm sweepin' my floor.
I'm crossin' my fingers and countin' every kiss,
And prayin' that it keeps on goin' on like this, 'cause I...
(To Chorus:)

I Love You This Much

Words and Music by
Chris DuBois, Don Sampson
and Jimmy Wayne

I'm from the Country

Words and Music by
Marty Brown, Richard Young
and Stan Webb

© 1998 BUG MUSIC, HIGH & DRY MUSIC (BMI), THEM YOUNG BOYS MUSIC (ASCAP)/Administered by BUG MUSIC
and STAN WEBB MUSIC/Administered by MCS AMERICA, INC.
All Rights Reserved   Used by Permission

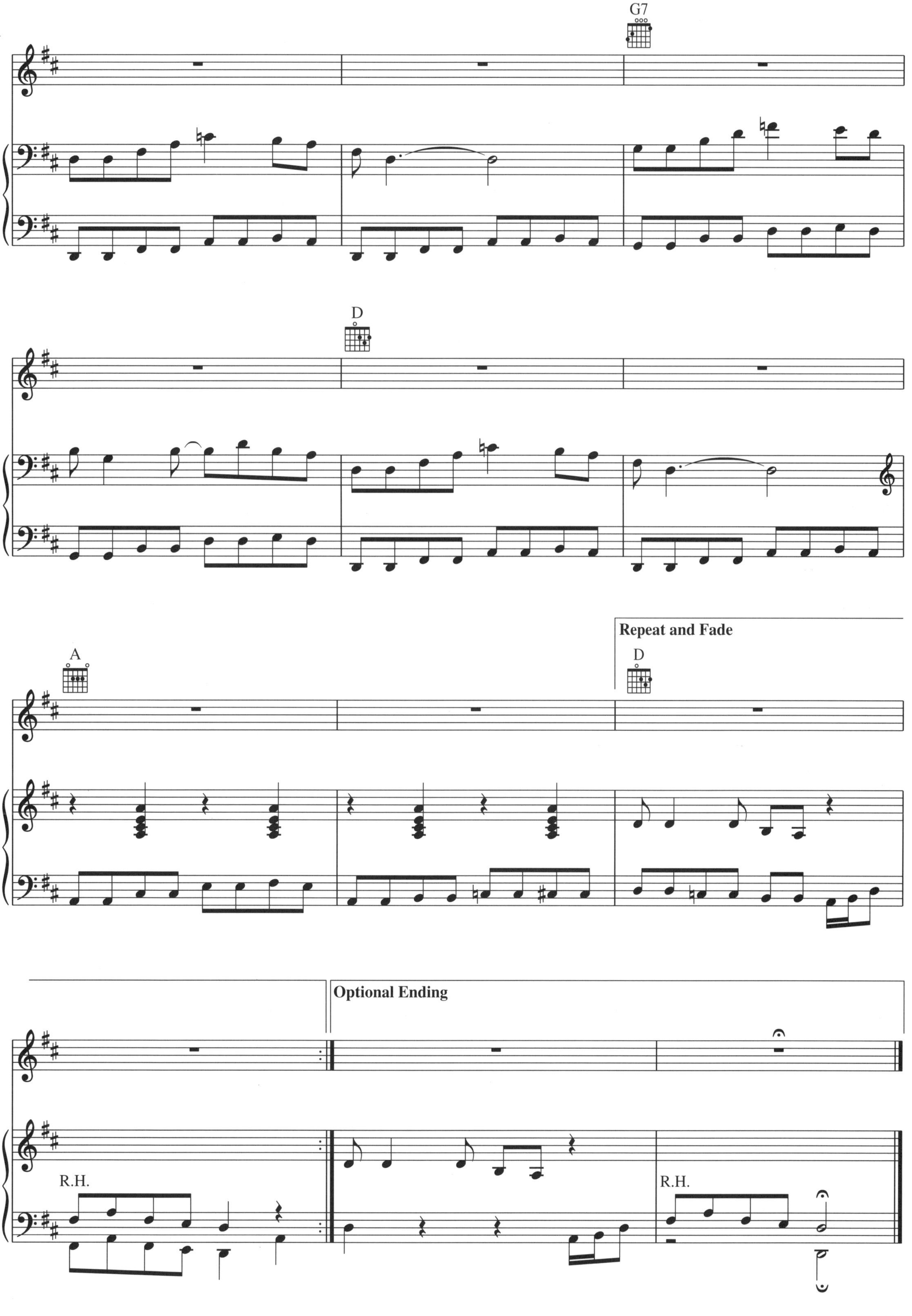
G7
D
Repeat and Fade
A
D
Optional Ending
R.H.
R.H.

Let's Make Love

Words and Music by
Bill Luther, Aimee Mayo,
Chris Lindsey and Marv Green

Moderately

(Female:) Baby, I've been drifting away, dreaming all day of holding you, touching you.

Copyright © 1999 by Careers-BMG Music Publishing, Inc., Songs Of Nashville DreamWorks,
Warner-Tamerlane Publishing Corp. and Golden Wheat Music
All Rights for Songs Of Nashville DreamWorks Administered by Cherry River Music Co.
All Rights for Golden Wheat Music Administered by Warner-Tamerlane Publishing Corp.
International Copyright Secured   All Rights Reserved

The on-ly thing I wan-na do is be with you, as close to you as I can be. And let's make love all night long un-til all our strength is gone.

E♭
B♭
And hold on tight, just let
F
Gm
go. I wan - na feel you in my soul.
E♭
Cm7
B♭/D
E♭
F
Un - til the sun comes up, let's make
B♭
F/A
Gm
B♭/F
love.
3

41

Look in my eyes, let's get lost tonight in each other. *Both:* Let's make love all night long until all our strength is gone. Hold on tight, just let

42

43

CODA
Am7
G/B
C
(Female:) Oh,
til the sun comes up,
(Female:) un -
Am7
G/B
Csus2
Dsus
til the sun comes up,
Both: let's make
G
D/F♯
love.
3
Em
Csus2
G
(Male:) all night long,
(Female:) Let's make love all night long. Let's make love.
rit.

Maybe We Should Just Sleep on It

Words and Music by
Jerry Laseter and Kerry Kurt Phillips

Moderately fast

I got an emp-ty feel-ing when that mov-ing van pulled up.
I'll pay them boys to stop right now and leave that truck out on the curb.

It got a whole lot emp-
The T-V and the phone's

ti - er as I watched them fill that truck.
packed up so we won't be dis - turbed.

And when they car - ried out your clothes it took my breath a - way.
There's not a light left in this room, just a shad - ow of a doubt.

Now they're head - ed for that bed. The
So let's make sure we don't give up be -

thought keeps run - nin' through my head.
fore we thought this through e - nough. Ba - by, may -

be we should just sleep on it to - night and

give our hearts just - a one more chance to change our minds.

I could be wrong but good-bye just don't feel right. So baby, may-

Cmaj7 / D♭maj7 *D / E♭* *To Coda* *Cmaj7 / D♭maj7*

1. be we should just sleep on it to-night.

2. *D.S. al Coda* be we should just sleep on it to-night.

Coda

be, ba - by, may - be, ba - by, may - be we should just sleep on it to - night.

Repeat and fade

Meat & Potato Man

Written by
John Pennell and Harley Allen

Moderately fast

I like my steak well done, my taters fried, football games on Monday night. It's just
fishin' holes, lightnin' bugs, Flatt 'n' Scruggs, and my woman's love. It's just

© 2000 SOLARGRASS MUSIC (BMI)/Administered by BUG MUSIC and COBURN MUSIC INC. (BMI)
All Rights Reserved   Used by Permission

G7 | who I am, ___ a meat and pota - to ___ man. ___
C | who I am, ___ a meat and pota - to ___ man. ___

G I like my **C** cof - fee black, ___ ol' ___ **F** T - V shows,
I like my Wran - gler jeans, ___ cow - boy boots,

C my wom - en hot, and my beer ___ ice ___ cold. ___ It's just
corn - bread and beans, and coun - try ___ roots. ___ It's just

G7 who I am, ___ a meat and pota - to ___ man. ___
who I am, ___ a meat and pota - to ___ man. ___

Lyrics:

I don't like cav-i-ar, su-shi bars, the I-R-S, or pho-ny stars. I'm a Hag-gard fan, a meat and po-ta-to man.

I don't like pol-i-tics, hyp-o-crites, folks with poo-dles dressed like kids. I'm a hound-dog fan, a meat and po-ta-to man.

I like my

Hey, that's just what I am, a meat and po-ta-to man.

My Maria

Words and Music by
Daniel J. Moore and B.W. Stevenson

Moderately

My Ma-ri-a,
- a,

don't you know I've come a long, long way?
there were some blue and sor-rowed times.

I've been long-in' to see her. When she's a-round,
Just my thoughts a-bout you bring back

Copyright © 1973 UNIVERSAL MUSIC CORP., SONGS OF UNIVERSAL, INC. and PROPHECY PUBLISHING, INC.
Copyright Renewed
All Rights Controlled and Administered by UNIVERSAL MUSIC CORP.
All Rights Reserved   Used by Permission

she takes my blues a - way. Sweet Ma - ri -
my peace of mind. Gyp - sy la -

- a,
- dy, the sun - light sure - ly hurts my eyes.
you're a mir - a - cle work for me.

I'm a lone - ly dream -
You set my soul

- er on a high - way in the skies.
free like a ship sail - in' on the sea.

Eb 3 fr
Bb
Ab 4 fr
Ma - ri -
Eb 3 fr
Ab 4 fr
Bb
Ab 4 fr
Eb 3 fr
- a, Ma -
Bb
Ab 4 fr
Eb 3 fr
Ab 4 fr
Eb 3 fr
ri, Ma - ri - a, I love you.
Bb
Ab 4 fr

My Ma-ri- / She is the sunlight when the skies are grey. She treats me so right. Lady, take me away.

My Ma-ri-a, Ma-ri, Ma-ri-a, I love you. My Ma-ri-

Repeat and Fade

Not a Day Goes By

Words and Music by
Steve Diamond and Maribeth Derry

Moderately slow

Got a picture of you ____ I carry in ____ my heart. ____
Close my eyes to see ____ it ____ when the world gets ____ dark. ____ Got a
wait for the phone ____ in the mid-dle of ____ the night, ____
think-in' you might call ____ me ____ if your dreams don't turn out ____ right. ____ And it

* Recorded a half step lower.

Copyright © 2001 American Broadcasting Music, Inc. (ASCAP)
All Rights Reserved

| G | D/F# | Em |

mem - 'ry of you ___ I car - ry in ___ my soul. ___
still a - maz - es me that I lie here in ___ the dark, ___

| C | G/B | Dsus4 | D | G/B |

I wrap it close a - round ___ me ___ when the nights get cold. ___
wish - in' you were next ___ to ___ me with your head a - gainst my heart. ___

| C | G/B | C |

If you asked me how I'm do - in', I'd say, "Just fine." ___

| G/B | Dsus4 | D |

But the truth is, ba - by, ___ if you could read ___ my mind, ___ not a day goes by that I don't think of you. After all this time, you're still with me, it's true. Somehow you remain locked so deep inside. Baby, baby, oh, baby, not a day goes

1. Em G/B C Dsus4
2. G
by. I still by.
f
D G C
Min - utes turns to ho - urs and the ho - urs to days.
D C D
Seems it's been for - ev - er that I've felt this way.
Not a
mf
Em G/B C Dsus4 D
day goes by that I don't think of you. Af - ter

Em G/B C Dsus4 D
all this time, you're still with me, it's true, oh.
f
Bm C G G/B C
Some - how you re - main locked so deep in - side.
F G/F F D
Tacet
Ba - by, ba - by, oh, ba - by, not a day goes by
Em G/B C Dsus4 D7 G
that I don't think of you.
dim.
rit.
mp

Not That Different

Written by
Joie Scott and Karen Taylor-Good

Slowly, in 2

She said, "We're much too dif-f'rent; we're from two sep-'rate worlds." And he ad-
she could hard-ly ar-gue with his pure and sim-ple log-ic. But

mit-ted she was part-ly right. But in his heart's
log-ic nev-er could con-vince a heart. She had al-

© 1996 SPOOFER MUSIC (BMI)/Administered by BUG MUSIC, K.T. GOOD MUSIC (SESAC) and W.B.M. MUSIC CORP. (SESAC)
All Rights for K.T. GOOD MUSIC Administered by W.B.M. MUSIC CORP.
All Rights Reserved   Used by Permission

Gadd9
__ de - fense, he told __ her what they had in com - mon was
ways dreamed of lov - ing some - one more ex - ot - ic, and

D   **A7sus4**   **A7**
strong e - nough __ to bond __ them for life.   He said, "Look __
he just did - n't seem to fit the part.   So she searched __

Cadd9   **D**
__ be - hind __ your own __ soul, and the per - son that you'll see __
__ for green - er pas - tures but nev - er could for - get __

G   **A7sus4**   **A**
just might re - mind __ you __ of me. __   I laugh, __
what he whis - pered when she left. __

D
Bm
G
I love,
I hope,
I try.
Asus4
A
D
Bm
I hurt,
I need,
I fear,
G
F#sus4
F#
G
I cry.
And I know you do the same things,
Esus4
E
G
To Coda
too.
So we're real - ly not that dif - f'rent,

67

tears fell at his feet, she didn't say "I love you." What she said meant even more. I laugh,

D.S. al Coda

Coda
no, we're really not that diff'rent, me and you.

She's Taken a Shine

Words and Music by
Richard Michael Bach and Greg Barnhill

Moderately fast

Rosie never was one for turning heads; she was just always kinda there.
Rosie hardly ever missed a bit of work; never took vacation days.

Copyright © 1996 DreamWorks Songs (ASCAP), Mike Chapman Publishing Enterprises (ASCAP),
Bayou Liberty Music (ASCAP), EMI Full Keel Music (ASCAP)
All Rights for DreamWorks Songs Administered by Cherry Lane Music Publishing Company, Inc.
All Rights for Mike Chapman Publishing Enterprises and Bayou Liberty Music Administered by Music & Media International, Inc.
International Copyright Secured All Rights Reserved

She had a few nice features more or less, no red ribbons in her hair.
Home or the diner, it was all the same to her; she didn't know any other way.

Since that Jesse's been coming to the diner, folks are saying that she's never looked finer.
But each afternoon now she starts to come alive; 'cause Jesse's there each day to pick her up at five.

She's got a diff'rent air.
You ought to hear them say:

She's taken a shine

70

to him, be-com-ing the wom-an that she's nev-er been. All of the guys are wish-ing they had-n't been so blind. She's tak-en a shine to life; now there's a spar-kle in her eyes. They all missed a gem, a dia-mond with-in; she's tak-en a shine.

Oh, what a lit-tle love can do.

Now that she's

D
Eb
Esus4
Fsus4
E
F
D.S. al Coda
found her-self, she's strong-er than she ev-er knew. She's tak-en a shine
D
E
A
D
E
Coda
Eb
F
Bb
Eb
F
she's tak-en a shine.
A
D
E
A
D
Bb
Eb
F
Bb
Eb
She's tak-en a shine.
E
F#m
D
E
E/G#
A
F
Gm
N.C.
Eb
F
F/A
Bb

Paint Me a Birmingham

Words and Music by
Buck Moore and Gary Duffy

Moderately slow

*sitting there,_ his brush in hand,_
looked at me_ with knowing eyes,_ then

painting waves_ as_ they danced_ upon the sands._ With
took a canvas from_ a bag_ there by his side._ Picked

*Recorded a half step lower.

Copyright © 2004 Songs of Nashville DreamWorks (BMI), Princetta Music (BMI), Brewbear Music Works (BMI) and Mama's House Music (BMI)
Worldwide Rights for Songs of Nashville DreamWorks and Princetta Music Administered by Cherry River Music Co.
International Copyright Secured   All Rights Reserved

ev-'ry stroke he brought to life the
up a brush and said to me, "Son,

deep blue of the o - cean a - gainst the morn-ing sky. I
just where in this pic - ture would you like to be?" And

asked him if he on - ly paint - ed o - cean scenes. He
I said, "If there's an - y way you can, could you

said, "for twen - ty dol - lars, I'll paint you an - y - thing." Could you paint me a
paint me back in - to her arms a - gain?"

Bir-ming-ham? Make it look just the way I planned. A lit-tle house on the edge of town, porch go-ing all the way a-round. Put her there in the front yard swing, cot-ton dress; make it ear-ly spring. For a while she'll be mine a-gain if you can paint me a Bir-ming-ham.

*From this point, recorded a half step higher than written.

He ___ Paint me a ___ if you can paint me a Bir-ming-ham. ___ Oh, paint me a Bir-ming-ham. ___

rit.

She's Got It All

Words and Music by
Peter Drew Womack and Craig Wiseman

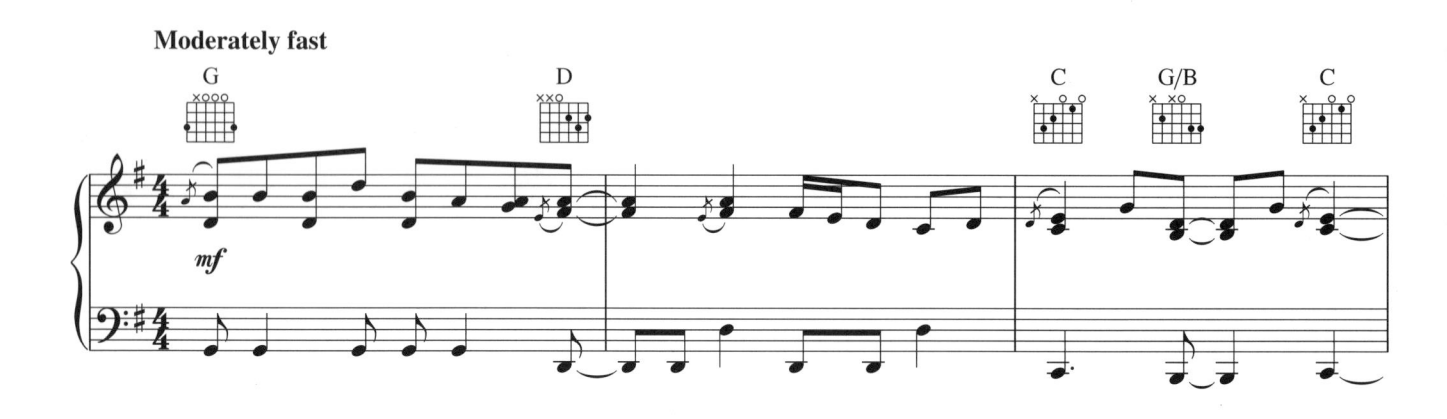

Moderately fast

She's got ev-'ry qual-i-ty from A all the way to Z. It's easy to see
You know that I ad-mit that some-one to love like this on-ly ex-ist-

Copyright © 1997 DreamWorks Songs (ASCAP), Daddy Rabbit Music (ASCAP),
Almo Music Corporation (ASCAP), EMI Full Keel Music (ASCAP) and Womaculate Conception (ASCAP)
Worldwide Rights for DreamWorks Songs Administered by Cherry Lane Music Publishing Company, Inc.
International Copyright Secured   All Rights Reserved

| D | Csus2 |

_____ she's the per - fect girl. _____
ed in _____ my prayers. _____

| G | D |

She's got ev - 'ry sin - gle _____ thing _____
Un - til I saw _____ her _____ face,

| G | C |

that makes up my wild - est _____ dreams. _____
I knew I'd found _____ the _____ place

| G | D | Csus2 | G/B |

Some - times I still _____ can't quite _____ be - lieve _____ she's hold - ing me, _____
where I could keep _____ my ev - 'ry faith _____ e - ter - nal - ly, _____

79

Am7add4
3fr
D
G
D
'cause she's got it all ___ of my heart, my soul, my ___ wish - es. All ___
Em
C
G
___ of my love, my hugs, my kiss - es. Ev - er - y - thing that
D
Em
C
D
means an - y - thing at all. ___ All ___
G
D/F♯
Em
___ of my life I've ___ spent ___ hop - in' I ___ could give some - one

such de-vo-tion. Ev-er-y sweet mem-o-ry I can re-call.

She's got it all.

(Lyrics)

All of my life I've spent hopin' I could give someone such devotion. Every sweet memory I can recall._

G/B D G D
All of my heart, my soul, my wish - es. All
Em C G
of my love, my hugs, my kiss - es. Ev - er - y sweet mem - o -
D C D
ry I can re - call. She's got it all.
G D Em C
She's got it all.

She's My Kind of Rain

Words and Music by
Robin Lerner and Tommy Lee James

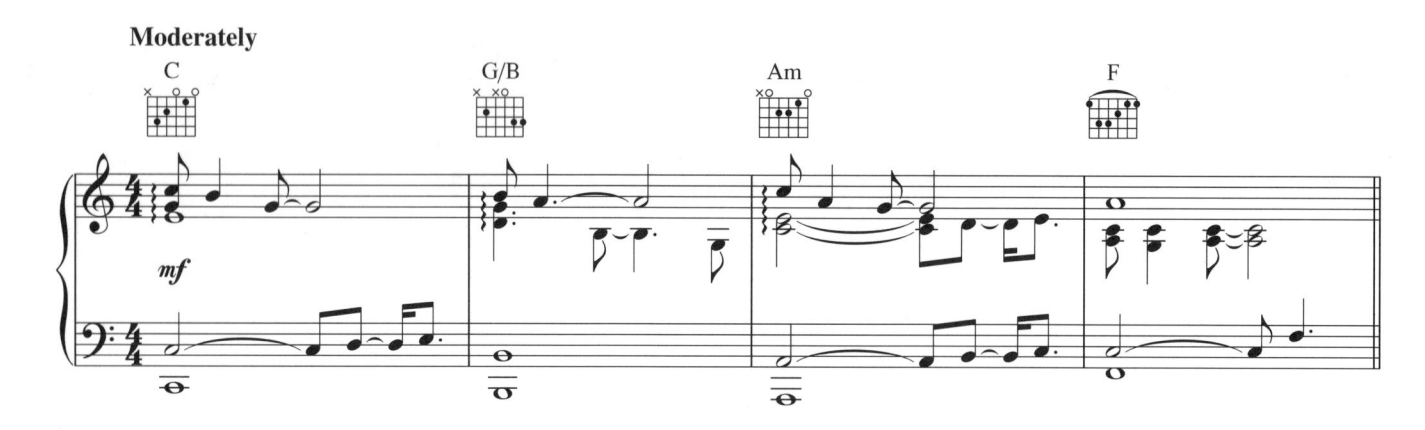

Moderately

She's my kind of rain, ___ like love in a drunk-en sky.
She's the sun-set's shad - ow. She's like Rem-brandt's light.

She's con-fet-ti fall-ing down all night.
She's the his-to-ry ___ that's made at night.

Copyright © 2002 Massabielle Music (BMI), Still Working For The Man, Inc. (BMI) and Tommy Lee James Songs (BMI)
Worldwide Rights for Massabielle Music Administered by Cherry River Music Co. and Songs Of DreamWorks
All Rights for Still Working For The Man, Inc. and Tommy Lee James Songs Administered by ICG
International Copyright Secured   All Rights Reserved

She sits quietly there, black water in a jar,
She's my lost companion. She's my dreaming tree
says, "Baby, why are you trembling like you are?" So I
together in this brief eternity. Summer

wait and I try. I confess like a child.
days, winter snow. She's all things to behold.
wait and I try. I confess all my crimes.

She's my kind of rain, like love in a drunken

To Coda
C G Dm7 F C G Dm7
sky. Con - fet - ti fall - ing down all night.
1.
F C G/B
She's my kind of rain.
Am F
2.
F
She's my kind of
C G/B Am
rain.

So I

She's my kind of rain.

She's my kind of rain.

Repeat and fade

Smile

Words and Music by
Chris Lindsey and Keith Follesé

Moderately slow

I still re-mem-ber the night we met.
Kiss me once for the good times, ba-by.

You said you loved my smile.
Kiss me twice for good-bye.

But your love for me was like a sum-mer breeze.
You can't help how you don't feel,

Oh, it last-ed for a while.
and it does-n't mat-ter why.

Copyright © 1998, 1999 Songs Of Nashville DreamWorks (BMI), Music Of Windswept (ASCAP) and Follazoo Music (ASCAP)
Worldwide Rights for Songs Of Nashville DreamWorks Administered by Cherry River Music Co.
Rights for Follazoo Music Administered by Music Of Windswept
International Copyright Secured All Rights Reserved

Em
Bm
I could hold on a lit - tle tight - er, I know. But when you
Give me a chance to bow out grace - ful - ly,
C
D7sus4
D7
love some - one, you got - ta let 'em go. So I'm gon - na smile,
'cause that's how I want you to re - mem - ber me. I'm gon - na smile,
G
D/G
C
'cause I wan - na make you hap - py.
mf
G
D/G
C
B7
B7/D♯
Laugh, so you can't see me cry. I'm gon - na

let you go___ in style. And e-ven if___ it kills me

1.
I'm gon-na smile.___

2.
I'm gon-na smile.___

I'm gon-na smile,___ so___

you can find the cour-age. Laugh, so you won't see me hurt-in'. I'm gon-na let you go in style. And e-ven if it kills me I'm gon-na smile.

Stay Gone

Words and Music by
Jimmy Wayne and Billy Kirsch

Moderately

Lyrics:
I've found ___ peace of mind. ___ I'm feel-ing good ___ a-gain. I'm on the oth-er side, ___ back a-mong the liv-ing. ___ Ain't a cloud in ___ the sky. ___ All my

— love ___ you, ___ and I will for-ev-er. We can hide the truth. ___ We know each oth-er' bet-ter. ___ When we try to make it work, ___ we

Copyright © 2002 Nashville DreamWorks Songs (ASCAP), Paper Angels Music (ASCAP), Sunchaser Music (ASCAP) and Kidbilly Music LLC (BMI)
Worldwide Rights for Nashville DreamWorks Songs, Paper Angels Music
and Sunchaser Music Administered by Cherry Lane Music Publishing Company, Inc.
International Copyright Secured   All Rights Reserved

tears have been cried. And I can fi- nal- ly
both end up hurt. And it ain't sup-posed to be that

say: Ba- by, ba- by, stay,
way. So, ba- by, ba- by, stay

right where you are. Like it this way. It's

good for my heart. I have-n't felt like this in

God knows how long. I know ev-'ry-thing's gonna be o-kay

1. if you just stay gone.

2. I still if you just stay gone.

When we try to make it work,

we both end up hurt. And love ain't sup-posed to be that way.

So, ba-by, ba-by,

if you just stay gone.

I know ev-'ry-thing's gon-na be o-kay if you just stay gone.

This Used to Be Our Town

Words and Music by
Chris Lindsey, Denny Carr and Jason McCoy

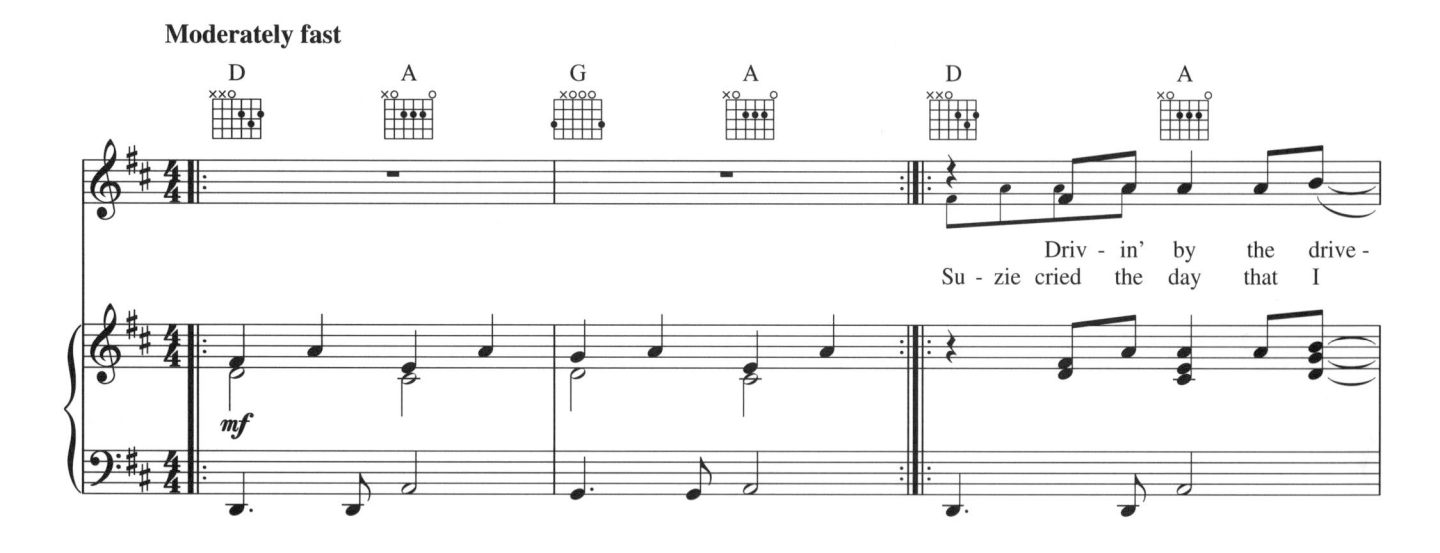

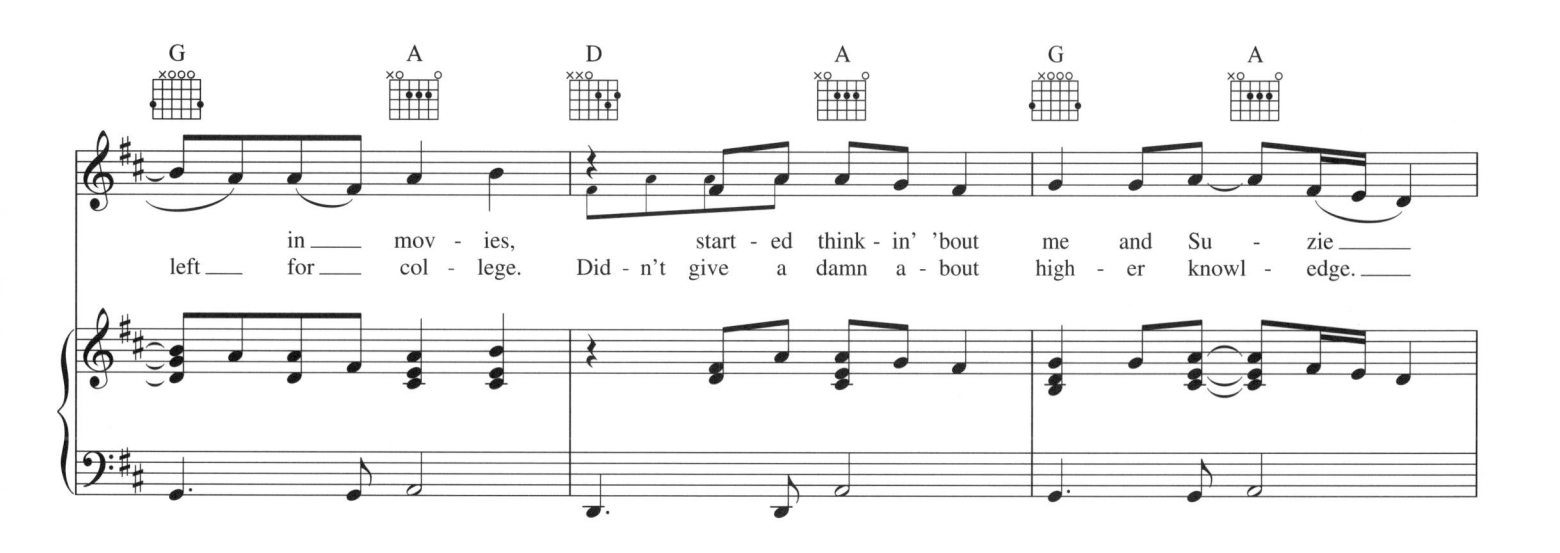

Moderately fast

Drivin' by the drive-in movies, started thinkin' 'bout me and Suzie and how we used to spend those Saturday nights.

Suzie cried the day that I left for college. Didn't give a damn about higher knowledge. All she really wanted was a family.

Copyright © 1995 Songs of DreamWorks (BMI), Airstrip Music, Inc. (SOCAN) and EMI Longitude Music (BMI)
Worldwide Rights for Songs of DreamWorks Administered by Cherry River Music Co.
International Copyright Secured   All Rights Reserved

| G/B | A | D | A | G | A |

Lat-er on we'd be out cruis-in',
When I got back there was noth-in' I could do.

| D | A | G | A | D | A |

dash-board drum-min' to our fa-v'rite mu-sic, kiss-in' on the porch till her
Her first ba-by was al-most two. I guess she's do-in'

| G | A7 | A7sus4 | A7 |

ma-ma flashed the light.
fine with-out me. Now,

| Em | D/F# | G | Em | D/F# | G |

We had the world in the palm of our hands. I guess fate had oth-
some things change and some things don't. Some things wait and some

er plans. / things won't. This used to be our town. There wasn't a back road we hadn't been down. This used to be our town. Every inch is still sacred ground. Now I'm drivin' these streets and her sweet memory still makes my heart pound. This used to be our town.

This used to be our town.

Now I'm driv-in' these streets_ and her sweet_ mem-o-ry_ still makes my_ heart pound._ This used to be our town._ This used to be our town._

Repeat and fade

You Are

Words and Music by
Jimmy Wayne, Chris Lindsey,
Aimee Mayo and Marv Green

Ba - by, when I look at you, you know it breaks my heart in two. How

Copyright © 2003 Nashville DreamWorks Songs (ASCAP), Monkey Feet Music (ASCAP), Paper Angels Music (ASCAP),
Sunchaser Music (ASCAP), Warner-Tamerlane Publishing Corp. (BMI), Golden Wheat Music (BMI),
Careers-BMG Music Publishing, Inc. (BMI) and Silverkiss Music Publishing (BMI)
Worldwide Rights for Nashville DreamWorks Songs, Monkey Feet Music, Paper Angels Music
and Sunchaser Music Administered by Cherry Lane Music Publishing Company, Inc.
U.S. Rights for Silverkiss Music Publishing Administered by Careers-BMG Music Publishing, Inc.
International Copyright Secured   All Rights Reserved

D	A
beau - ti - ful you are.	I've seen you in a mil - lion dreams.

E	Bm	A/C#
Now you're fi - n'lly here with me.		We will

D	Gmaj9
nev - er be a - part.	I wan - na hold you for - ev -

A	Gmaj7
- er.	That's all I'll ev -

-er need. You are my love. You are my life, my heart and soul; the truest friend I've ever known. You are my world, all of my dreams, my fantasy, my reality. I love ev'rything you

are. Yes, I do.

Ev-'ry time I close my eyes, it hits me so deep in-side. How real this feel-ing is. I'm in-tox-i-cat-ed by your touch.

E/G♯
Bm
A/C♯
It's a sweet, sweet rush. I'm in
D
Gmaj9
love with your kiss. You're the one that I
A
Gmaj9
A
D.S. al Coda I
trust the most. You changed me.
Coda I
A
G♯m
4fr
al - i - ty. I love ev - 'ry - thing you are.

al - i - ty. I love ev-'ry-thing you are.

Ev'ry-thing, I love ev-'ry-thing you are.

Your Everything
(I Want to Be Your Everything)

Words and Music by
Chris Lindsey and Bob Regan

Moderately slow

[Verse 1]
The first time I looked in your eyes, I knew that I would do anything for you. The first time you touched my face

[Verse 2]
want to give back what you've given to me. And I want to witness all of your dreams. Now that you've shown me who I

[Verse 3]
When you wake up I'll be the first thing you see. And when it gets dark you can reach out to me. I'll cherish your words, and I'll fin-

Copyright © 1999 Songs Of Nashville DreamWorks (BMI), BMG Songs, Inc. (ASCAP) and Yessiree Bob Music (ASCAP)
Worldwide Rights for Songs Of Nashville DreamWorks Administered by Cherry River Music Co.
Worldwide Rights for Yessiree Bob Music Administered by BMG Songs, Inc.
International Copyright Secured   All Rights Reserved

Dmaj7
E/D
A/E
E
I felt what I'd nev - er felt with
real - ly am, I wan - na be more than
ish your thoughts. And I'll be your com - pass, ba - by,
1.
2.
D/E
E
D/E
E
D/E
an - y - one else. I just your man.
when you get lost.
I wan - na
A
A/C#
be the wind that fills your sail, and be the hand that lifts your veil,
mf
Dadd9
2fr
E
and be the moon that moves your tides, the sun com-ing up in your eyes.

A Be the wheel that nev-er rusts, **A/C#** and be the spark that lights you up,

Dadd9 all that you've been dream-ing of and **G** more, so much

D/F# more. **D** I wan-na be your **A** *To Coda* ev-'ry-thing. **E/A**

D/A **E/A** **F#m** **E/F#** **Esus4** *D.S. (take 2nd ending) al Coda*

Coda

ev - 'ry-thing.

I'll be the wheel that nev - er rusts. And be the spark that lights you up.

All that you've been dream-ing of and more, so much

more. I wan-na be your ev-'ry-thing.

I wan-na be your ev-'ry-thing.

I wan-na be your ev-'ry-thing.

Repeat and fade